Spotter's Guide to
ROCK
MINERALS

Alan Woolley

Special Consultant
Charles Fray
Associate Professor of Marine Science,
Dowling College, Oakdale, New York

Photography by Mike Freeman

SCHOLASTIC INC.
New York Toronto London Auckland Sydney

Contents

ISBN 0-590-73870-4

First published in Great Britain in 1978 by Usborne Publishing Ltd. Copyright © 1978/1985 by Usborne Publishing Ltd. All rights reserved. Published by Scholastic Inc., 555 Broadway, New York, NY 10012, by arrangement with Usborne Publishing Limited.

15 14 13 12 11 10 9 8   2 3 4 5 6 / 0

Printed in the U.S.A.   23

First Scholastic printing, January 1996

How to use this book

This book tells you how to recognize some of the rocks, minerals and fossils that you will find. There is a section in the book on each of these three things. Each section has its own short introduction, which explains what rocks, minerals and fossils are, and how to find and identify them.

When you find a specimen, or see one in a collection, try to decide whether it is a rock or a mineral, and then compare it with the photographs in the correct section. The captions will give you more information to help you identify it in other ways, so read them carefully and make any test that they suggest.

If you do not understand any of the words, then look them up in the glossary on page 61, or in the index at the end of the book.

When you have identified your find, check it off in the little circle next to the correct caption.

You can also enter your score in

Check off each rock, mineral, or fossil

	SCORE	DATE SEEN
Agate	15	

the scorecard on pages 62 and 63, for having seen or found the specimen. If you go on an outing and see many different rocks, minerals and fossils (in a museum, for instance), you can then add up your total score for the day.

Where to look

The best places to look for rocks, minerals and fossils are areas where the earth has been disturbed or worn away by water or wind. Sea cliffs, dried out riverbeds, excavations, roadsides, fields, and even gardens are all good places to search for rocks. Be very careful if you visit any of these places, and never go near overhanging rocks, nor try to climb rock faces. Ask permission before taking rocks from land which is privately owned.

Old quarries can be very dangerous, and if they are still being worked, you will not be allowed

near the area, so it is better to collect your samples elsewhere.

Wherever you live, you will be able to find some of the rocks and minerals shown in this book. However, some types are quite rare, so look for them in exhibitions, and try to find museums with good collections.

What to take

Before you set off, read the section on page 58 which tells you what equipment you will need, and how to fill in your rockhound's notebook.

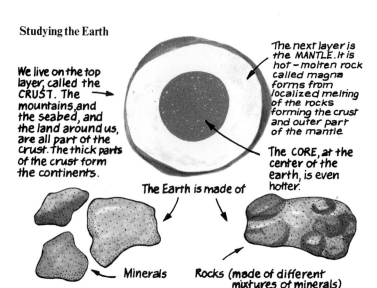

The next layer is the MANTLE. It is hot – molten rock called magma forms from localized melting of the rocks forming the crust and outer part of the mantle

We live on the top layer, called the CRUST. The mountains, and the seabed, and the land around us, are all part of the crust. The thick parts of the crust form the continents.

The CORE, at the center of the earth, is even hotter.

The Earth is made of

Minerals

Rocks (made of different mixtures of minerals)

This diagram shows the different layers that make up the earth.

People who study these layers, and the rocks and minerals they are made of, are called **geologists.** They try to find out how the earth was formed, how it is changing and the things that affect its structure. Most of what they know comes from studying the earth's **crust.** The other layers are too deep inside the earth to be seen directly.

What are minerals?

Rocks are made either of one mineral, or, more often, a mixture of minerals, so it is important to know something about minerals before you start looking at rocks.

Minerals are made of **elements.** Elements are simple substances that cannot be broken down into any other substance. Some minerals, such as gold, are made of only one element. But most minerals are made of two or more elements.

The name of an element can be written as a combination of letters called a **symbol:** for instance, sodium is Na and chlorine is Cl.

Salt is made of sodium and chlorine, and can be written as the **formula** NaCl.

Many minerals are made of a large number of elements, so their formulae are very complicated. We have not given the formulae in this book, but if you want to find out what they are, look in some of the books listed on page 60.

People value and search for minerals because many of them are useful. For instance, we get some asbestos, which is used to make things fireproof, from a mineral called serpentine; and the "lead" inside pencils is really a mineral called graphite, mixed with clay.

How to recognize minerals

1. Shape

Often minerals are found as shape-less lumps; such pieces are called **"massive"**. But minerals can also form special, recognizable shapes that can help you to identify them.

When the elements that the mineral is made of get built up in layers on the mineral's outside surfaces, the mineral is said to "grow". Usually minerals grow into all sorts of rough shapes in the spaces between the other minerals around them. But if a mineral can grow freely (on the seabed, for instance, or in a hole in a rock), it may form beautiful, regular shapes with flat surfaces. These shapes are called **crystals,** and each mineral has a range of crystal shapes which it always forms.

Look on page 56 for some typical crystal shapes, and also next to some of the photographs.

Minerals also form special shapes which are not crystals. For instance, the mineral hematite often forms smoothly rounded masses which are kidney shaped. Some minerals, like smithsonite, form rounded crusts on rocks and other minerals. Others, like pyrite, may form smoothly rounded lumps called nodules.

These special shapes are described in the captions to some of the pictures.

If you find a mineral with perfectly flat surfaces, it is probably a crystal. However, some minerals break cleanly when hit, leaving pieces with smooth surfaces that look like crystals.

These clean breaks are called **"cleavages"**, and each mineral tends to break or "cleave" more easily in

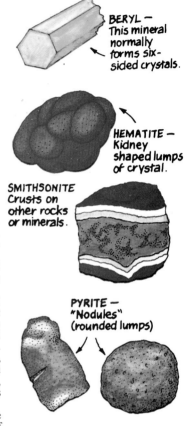

BERYL — This mineral normally forms six-sided crystals.

HEMATITE — Kidney shaped lumps of crystal.

SMITHSONITE Crusts on other rocks or minerals.

PYRITE — "Nodules" (rounded lumps)

some directions than in others. The way it breaks is called its cleavage pattern (some are shown on page 57 and also next to the photographs).

You can often identify minerals by a combination of their crystal shape and cleavage pattern.

2. Color and Streak

Few minerals are always the same shade, and some vary a great deal in color. Quartz, for instance, can be white, yellow, red, violet, brown, and other colors too. However, when minerals have been powdered the color does not vary. The best way to powder a mineral is to draw it firmly over a white, unglazed tile. The powder mark it makes is called a **"streak"**. Most minerals always make the same color streak. Find out from the captions what colors to look for. If the mineral is harder than the tile (probably about 7 – see below) it will not streak.

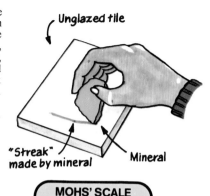

Unglazed tile

"Streak" made by mineral

Mineral

3. Hardness

The captions also often give a "hardness" number in a range from one to ten. This is another way of identifying an unknown mineral.

Minerals differ widely in how hard they are, but their hardness can be estimated, by using a list called **Mohs' scale.** This list names ten minerals in order of their hardness, starting with talc (the softest) and ending with diamond (the hardest).

If you draw a sharp corner of one mineral over another, and it makes a scratch mark, then you will know that the material with the scratch on it is the softer.

By using a set of the standard minerals of Mohs' scale (which can be bought quite cheaply), you can test the hardness of the minerals you find.

Scratch the unknown mineral with the standard minerals, starting with the softer ones, until you get a mark. Then use your mineral to scratch the standard minerals. For instance, if the unknown mineral can be scratched by apatite, but is itself scratched by fluorite, then its hardness is said to be 4½.

If you don't have a set of standard

MOHS' SCALE
1 Talc
2 Gypsum
3 Calcite
4 Fluorite
5 Apatite
6 Orthoclase
7 Quartz
8 Topaz
9 Corundum
10 Diamond

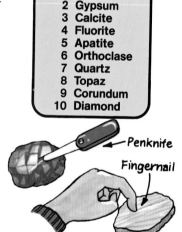

Penknife

Fingernail

minerals, you can use other things. The blade of a penknife has a hardness of about 5½, but use one only very carefully, and, if possible, wear gloves. Your fingernail has a hardness of about 2½, so it will scratch minerals like talc and gypsum. Minerals of a hardness greater than 6 will scratch glass.

Gold and Silver

◀ Gold

Usually found as tiny, deep yellow specks. Also forms larger lumps called "nuggets." It occurs in igneous and sedimentary rocks. Can sometimes be gotten from river sands and gravels by "panning" (see picture). Hardness 2½-3, so softer than pyrite or chalcopyrite (fool's gold). Streak gold-yellow. Used in jewelry and in coins. Because gold is rare, it has long been the symbol of power and riches. Many countries keep their savings in the form of gold bars.

Gold-bearing gravel is swirled around the bottom of a tin pan. The heavy gold sinks to the bottom. ➚

Silver ▶

Like gold, silver is one of the few metals sometimes found unmixed with other elements. It is malleable, that is, it can be hammered or squeezed into any shape. Silver forms wiry shapes and also small specks. It usually occurs in igneous rocks but is rather rare. Silver-white in color, but quickly tarnishes to black. Hardness 2½-3. Most silver is used in the making of photographic film. Also used for cutlery, trophies, jewelry, bowls, etc.

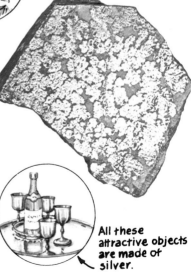

All these attractive objects are made of silver.

7

Graphite and Diamond

◀ Graphite

Graphite is made of the element carbon and is often found in certain kinds of schists and limestones. It makes flat crystals, but is more common as tiny grains. It is very soft, hardness 1-2. It feels greasy, and makes the fingers black. The name comes from a Greek word that means to write, and today it is still used for writing. The "lead" in pencils is not lead at all, but a mixture of clay and graphite.

It is the graphite in this pencil that marks the paper. ➙

Diamond ▶

Like graphite, diamond is made of carbon. It occurs mainly in the rock called kimberlite. If heated to a very high temperature, it will burn. It is the hardest mineral known, with a hardness of 10, and it will scratch glass. Used industrially for cutting very hard materials. The most prized diamonds are colorless and clear, but they may be yellow, brown, red or black. For jewelry, the crystals are "cut" by a craftsman. Natural uncut diamonds do not sparkle.

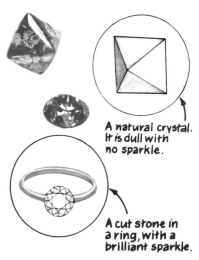

A natural crystal. It is dull with no sparkle.

A cut stone in a ring, with a brilliant sparkle.

8

Sulfur and Pyrite

Sulphur ▶

Found in rocks near volcanoes and around hot springs. It usually makes a powdery crust on rocks, but also forms large crystals. If heated it will melt. Burns easily, with a strong unpleasant smell. Bright yellow in color, sometimes brownish. Streak white. Hardness 1½-2½. Mined by pumping very hot water down through pipes to melt it. It is then forced out by air pressure. Used to make insecticides, paper, matches and explosives.

A single, cube shaped pyrite crystal. Many have parallel lines on faces

A group of crystals

◀ Pyrite

A common mineral. Also called iron pyrites. Made of iron and sulfur, often as a result of the decay of animal and vegetable matter. In many fossils the original material has been replaced by pyrite. It often forms good crystals, particularly cubes. Also forms nodules in some rocks, such as shale and chalk. Occurs in rocks as irregular masses. Color pale brass-yellow. Streak greenish black. Hardness 6-6½. Harder than gold and a paler yellow. If struck sharply, it gives off sparks.

Chalcopyrite and Galena

Chalcopyrite ▶

Also called copper pyrites. Made of copper, iron and sulfur. Forms irregular lumps and sometimes crystals. Brass yellow color, but will tarnish and look iridescent (with many different colors, a bit like oil on water). Streak greenish black. Hardness 3½-4. Found in a wide range of igneous and metamorphic rocks. Differs from pyrite by its deeper color, tarnish and lower hardness. Harder than gold. Called "fool's gold."

◀ Galena

Made of the elements lead and sulfur. It often forms cube shaped crystals, which split easily into cube shaped pieces (see sketch). It is found in some sedimentary rocks, particularly as large masses in limestone. Has a dull gray color and streak, but when freshly broken is a shining silver-gray. It is very heavy. Hardness 2½. Galena is the most common mineral that contains lead. Lead is used in solder and paints, and was once used for water pipes.

If you hit a piece of galena with a hammer it will break into small, cube shaped pieces

Sphalerite and Arsenopyrite

◀ Sphalerite

Also known as zinc blende, blende and black jack. The name comes from a Greek word meaning treacherous. It can easily be mistaken for other minerals. Streak brown to light yellow to white. Color varies from yellow to brown to black. Sometimes transparent. Hardness 3½-4. Sphalerite often occurs with galena. It may form masses in limestone or be found in veins. It provides most of the world's zinc, which is widely used in industry.

Arsenopyrite ▶

Also has the strange name mispickel. It is made of iron, arsenic and sulfur. It may form good crystals, often with close parallel lines along the faces. Silver to gray-white, and may have a brownish tarnish. The streak is dark grayish black, with a metallic shine, like the blade of a knife. Hardness 5½-6. It is often found in veins with gold and quartz. When struck, it smells a bit like garlic.

Magnetite and Hematite

◀ Magnetite

An important ore of iron made of iron and oxygen. It forms crystals the same shape as the natural diamond crystal on page 8. Color and streak black. Hardness 5½-6½. It is strongly magnetic, so a good magnet picks it up and it makes a compass needle move. Magnetite was once used as a compass itself. If a long, thin piece, known as a lodestone, is hung freely on a thread it will point north/south when still.

A lodestone. Magnetism was known to the Chinese 3,000 years ago.

Hematite ▶

Sometimes spelled "haematite." It is also known as kidney ore because it often forms kidney shaped masses. It may be steel gray to black, but is often also dull to bright red. It has a red streak. Hardness 5½-6½. The name comes from the Greek word for blood. Hematite is the most important source of iron. It is also used as a polishing powder. It is widespread in sedimentary rocks and causes the red color of many rocks.

Corundum, Sapphire, Ruby

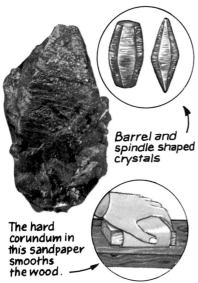

Barrel and spindle shaped crystals

The hard corundum in this sandpaper smooths the wood.

◄ Corundum

Made of aluminum and oxygen. Forms rough, six-sided, barrel and spindle shaped crystals. May be yellow, brown or green. Best known kinds are red (ruby) and blue (sapphire), both described below. It is very hard (9), second only to diamond in hardness, so it makes a good abrasive. Emery, used for grinding and sharpening, contains a lot of corundum. Found in some igneous and metamorphic rocks such as schists and gneisses.

Sapphire and Ruby ►

These are varieties of corundum. Corundum is called sapphire if it is a good blue color and transparent. If it is pink to blood-red and transparent, it is called ruby. Together with diamond and emerald, these are the most precious gemstones. Star sapphire and star ruby show a six-rayed star of light when a strong light is shone upon them. The best sapphires and rubies come from Burma and Sri Lanka.

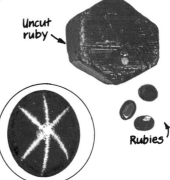

Uncut ruby

Rubies

A six-rayed star light from a star sapphire

Goethite and Pyrolusite

◀ Goethite

Crystals are rare. It often forms rounded lumps or long, sausagelike masses. Usually very dark brown, but may be yellow-brown. Streak brownish yellow. Hardness 5-5½. Goethite forms by the effect of water on minerals such as magnetite and pyrite. Because it nearly always forms by the alteration of other minerals, it is called a "secondary" mineral. Is sometimes mined for the iron in it. Its name comes from the German poet, Goethe, who collected minerals.

Pyrolusite ▶

Made of manganese and oxygen. Often forms fern-like shapes in sedimentary rocks. It also forms masses of thin, radiating crystals, hardness 6-6½. Large crystals are rare. Massive pyrolusite has a hardness of only 1-2. Color and streak black. Nodules are found at the bottom of the sea. In the future these may be collected for industrial use. They contain useful metals like copper, iron and nickel, as well as manganese.

← In the past, these fernlike shapes were often mistaken for fossils

Halite and Fluorite

Table salt is the same as halite.

◄ Halite
Also called "rock salt". Formed by the evaporation of sea water long ago. Layers in sedimentary rock are often hundreds of yards thick. When water is pumped into layers of halite, it dissolves and comes to the surface as brine (salty water). This is evaporated to give household salt. Usually massive, halite also makes single crystals, mainly cubes. Streak white. Hardness 2½. May be transparent or colorless; usually stained brown or yellow.

Fluorite ►
Also called fluorspar. Often forms good crystals, which are cubes. It may be a wide range of colors – blue, purple, green and yellow are common. Rarely white or pink. Often transparent. Streak white. Hardness 4. Common in mineral veins. The banded variety called "Blue John" has been used for carving since Roman times. Fluorite shines in ultraviolet light; this effect is called fluorescence after the mineral. Used in the chemical industry, and in smelting iron.

Calcite

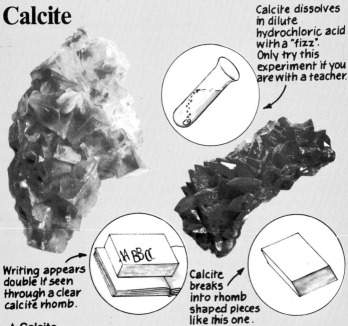

Calcite dissolves in dilute hydrochloric acid with a "fizz". Only try this experiment if you are with a teacher.

Writing appears double if seen through a clear calcite rhomb.

Calcite breaks into rhomb shaped pieces like this one.

▲ Calcite

This is made of calcium, carbon and oxygen. Its crystals are more variable in shape than those of any other mineral. When broken, it always forms six-sided shapes called rhombs. If you look through a clear rhomb placed over some writing on paper, you will see two groups of writing. Calcite is usually white, but can be gray, green, yellow, red or blue. Streak is white. Hardness 3. It dissolves with fizzing in dilute hydrochloric acid. Calcite will dissolve in slightly acidic water. It may re-form in layers around springs and eventually become sedimentary rock. It will also leave gritty deposits in cooking pots when the tap water is "hard".

Limestone and marble are made mostly of calcite. Impure marble may show a wide range of colors. Stalactites and stalagmites are formed when water containing calcite drips from the roofs of caves in limestone areas. Millions of tons of limestone are quarried every year to make cement, as a building stone, and also for surfacing roads.

Malachite and Smithsonite

◀ Malachite

A carbonate of copper. Forms crystals only rarely. Usually found as rounded masses, or in forms that look like bunches of grapes. The color is a bright green, and the streak pale green. Usually banded with circular or rounded patterns. Hardness 3½-4. It will dissolve and fizz in warm hydrochloric acid. A common mineral in copper deposits, particularly if these are in an area of limestone. It is often polished and used in jewelry.

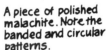

A piece of polished malachite. Note the banded and circular patterns.

Smithsonite ▶

A carbonate of zinc. Usually forms rounded masses and also crusts, coating other minerals and rocks. These masses and crusts are normally layered, showing how the mineral has been deposited. Displays a wide range of colors: white, gray, green, blue, yellow and brown. Streak white. Hardness 4-4½. Found in ore deposits containing zinc. Dissolves and fizzes in warm acids. (Never try this experiment unless you are with a teacher.)

Barite and Gypsum

◀ Barite

Good crystals are quite common. They tend to be white but may be brownish or reddish. Streak is white. It is often glassy looking and transparent. It is found in veins, often filling veins and holes in limestone. Hardness 2½-3½. Contains the element barium, which gives the bright green color in flares and fireworks. It is also used to make very heavy muds to pump down boreholes, so that pieces of drilled rock will float up and can then be examined.

Gypsum ▶

A common mineral, sometimes forming clear crystals called selenite. Also forms lumps of parallel fibers called satin spar. The fibers often run across small veins. Generally colorless or white, but may be yellowish when massive. Hardness only 2, so it can be scratched with a fingernail. Streak white. Occurs in sedimentary rocks, either as layers or veins. A lot of gypsum is mined and used in plaster, cements, paper and paint. Fine grained massive gypsum, called alabaster, is used for carving.

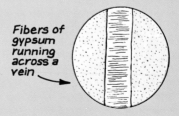

Fibers of gypsum running across a vein ➤

Apatite and Turquoise

Apatite ▶

Made mainly of the elements calcium, phosphorus and oxygen. It may be white, gray, greenish or bluish. Streak white. Hardness 5. Often occurs in six-sided crystals. Found in most igneous rocks such as granites, but in small amounts only. Also found in some metamorphic rocks. A sedimentary rock called phosphate rock is almost pure apatite and is mined for fertilizer. Fossil bones are mostly apatite. So are your teeth.

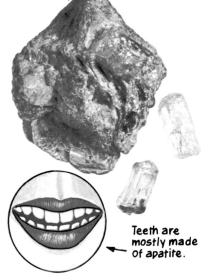

Teeth are mostly made of apatite.

◀ Turquoise

Made mainly of copper, aluminum and phosphorus. The copper causes the sky blue to apple green color in turquoise. Streak white to pale green. Hardness 5-6. Crystals are very rare. It usually forms masses, small veins and crusts. Found in hot, dry regions. The fine blue colored turquoise is prized as a semiprecious stone, and has been mined in Iran for thousands of years. The North American Indians used it for jewelry. Still widely used in rings, etc.

A polished piece of turquoise

Garnet and Tourmaline

Garnet ▶

There are many kinds of garnets. The elements are usually calcium, magnesium, aluminum and iron combined with silicon and oxygen. Color varies, but dark red and reddish brown are common. Often forms good crystals. Common in certain metamorphic rocks, schists and gneisses in particular. Garnet is used as an abrasive because it is hard (7-7½) and breaks into sharp, angular pieces. Glued to paper, it makes sandpaper. Some colored garnets are used in jewelry.

A cut garnet

There are several shapes of garnet crystals. This is an example of just one.

◀ Tourmaline

Makes long crystals that are triangular in cross-section, though the sides are slightly curved. A series of parallel lines usually runs along their length. They tend to be black, but blue, pink and green ones occur. A crystal may well show two different colors. Streak white. Hardness 7½. Tourmaline crystals are used in some kinds of pressure gauge, because when squeezed, they develop an electric charge. Often found in pegmatites. Transparent ones of good color are cut and polished as gemstones.

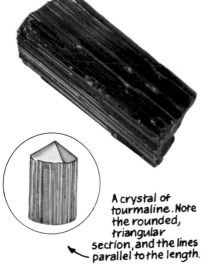

A crystal of tourmaline. Note the rounded, triangular section, and the lines parallel to the length.

Olivine and Serpentine

Olivine ▶

Olivine is made of magnesium, iron, silicon and oxygen. It usually forms granular masses, and only rarely good crystals. The color is normally olive green, but the kinds of olivine rich in magnesium are white, and those mostly of iron are black. The magnesium kind is found in metamorphosed limestone.

Transparent olivine of a good green color makes an attractive gemstone, and is called peridot. Hardness 6½-7. A common mineral in some basalts and gabbros.

◀ Serpentine

Found either as irregular lumps or as bundles of very thin fibers. The latter is known as asbestos; it can be a bit like cotton wool. Because of its fibers and the fact that it is not affected by heat or chemicals, it is used in making special cements and for fireproofing. Serpentine is usually green, but may be gray or yellow. The color is often variable and patchy. It has a waxy or greasy appearance. Hardness 2-5, usually 4. Easy to cut and carve, it is sometimes used as an ornamental stone.

Fibers of asbestos can be pulled out by hand ➤

Beryl, Emerald, Aquamarine

◄ Beryl

Made of the elements silicon, oxygen, aluminum and beryllium. Commonly forms long crystals with six sides. Color usually pale green, but can also be white and yellow. Streak white; hardness 8. Transparent, gem quality beryl may be dark or light green (emerald, see below), bluish green (aquamarine, see below), yellow (heliodor) or pink (morganite). Usualiy found in granite pegmatites*. Single crystals weighing over 100 tons have been found. Mined for beryllium, or for gems.

Emerald and Aquamarine ►

These are varieties of beryl. Transparent dark or light green stones are called emeralds. Flawless ones are very rare and valuable. The finest come from Muso in Colombia, where they occur in cavities in a limestone. The Colombian government strictly limits their supply. Aquamarine, the name for pale or greenish blue beryl, means "the color of the sea." Although very attractive, it is not as valuable as emerald.

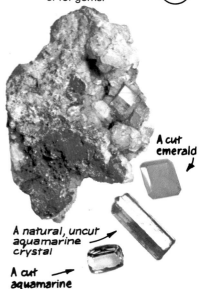

A cut emerald

A natural, uncut aquamarine crystal

A cut aquamarine

*see page 40

Augite and Hornblende

Augite ▶

Made principally of calcium, magnesium, aluminum and iron combined with silicon and oxygen. It forms stubby crystals with eight sides. The crystals cleave in two directions at right angles (see sketch). The color is black to dark green. Hardness 5½-6½.

Augite is found in all basalts and gabbros, and in other types of igneous rock as well. Quite large, well shaped crystals can sometimes be obtained from lavas and from tuffs.

This is what the cleavage pattern of augite looks like through a microscope.

◀ Hornblende

Made of a variety of elements, including sodium, calcium, magnesium, silicon, aluminum, oxygen and iron. It forms stubby or long six-sided crystals. They cleave in two directions which form angles of about 120° and 60° (see sketch). Compare this with augite. Color varies from green to black. Hardness 5-6. Found in a wide range of igneous and metamorphic rocks, and forms the greater part of the rock called amphibolite (page 48).

A hornblende crystal showing two cleavages, as seen through a microscope.

Mica and Talc

Mica ▶

Two main kinds: muscovite is white and silvery; biotite is black or brown and shiny. It forms "books" of very thin sheets or flakes. If separated with a knife blade or pin, the sheets are transparent, though biotite sheets are brown. Hardness 2-3. Both kinds are common in granites and pegmatites, also in schists. Muscovite has many uses in the electrical industry. It was once used for making windows in stoves and heaters.

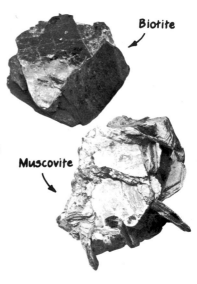

Biotite

Muscovite

◀ Talc

Made of magnesium, silicon, oxygen and hydrogen. It forms masses which may be layered. Usually pale green, but may be white or gray. It is the softest mineral on Mohs' scale (1) and can be easily scratched with a fingernail. Streak white. Has a soapy feel. Occurs in some metamorphic rocks. Some rocks, called soapstone or steatite, are made almost wholly of talc. It is used for making small carvings, and in porcelain, paper, talcum powder, face powder, paint and rubber.

Quartz

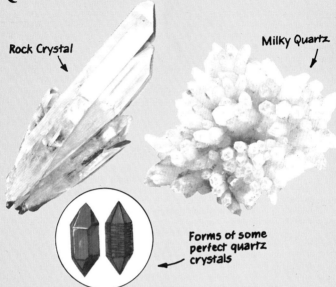

Rock Crystal

Milky Quartz

Forms of some perfect quartz crystals

Quartz

Made of silicon and oxygen. Common in many rocks and the most common mineral in sands. Good crystals are often found in cavities. Usually six-sided but they have many different kinds of faces at the end. Lines often run across side faces. A broken surface is smooth and curved. Quartz has a wide range of colors (see overleaf). Hardness 7. It has many uses in the cement and glass making and electrical industries and as an ornamental and semiprecious stone.

▲ Milky Quartz and Rock Crystal

The commonest variety of quartz is the opaque, white kind called milky quartz. It makes white veins which cut through metamorphic and igneous rocks; also in pegmatites. Clear, transparent quartz is called rock crystal. It is found as crystals or small, irregular lumps. Small crystals have sometimes been mistaken for diamonds. Sometimes carved, and has also been used for spectacles, lenses, and in radio sets.

Quartz

Amethyst ▶

Another variety of quartz. Its transparent color is usually uneven, varying from deep purple to pale blue, or even colorless. Usually found as well shaped crystals forming crusts, sometimes a yard or more across, lining holes in volcanic rocks. A popular, ornamental and semiprecious stone. Bishops traditionally wear an amethyst ring. There is an old belief that it protects the wearer from drunkenness.

A bishop's amethyst ring

Smoky Quartz

A Scottish pin

◀ Smoky Quartz and Citrine

Smoky quartz is transparent to semitransparent, and gray brown or nearly black. Sometimes called cairngorm after the mountains in Scotland where it may be found. It is often cut and polished and worn by Scotsmen with their national dress. Citrine is quartz which is yellow and transparent. Cut stones are often sold as topaz, which they resemble. Most citrine used in jewelry is made by heating amethyst until it turns yellow.

Chalcedony

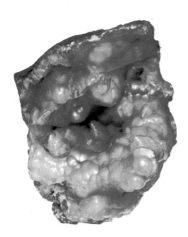

◀ Chalcedony

A variety of quartz which is very fine grained and does not form crystals. There are two kinds: chalcedony (one color); and agate (bands of different colors). Chalcedony usually forms rounded masses and sometimes occurs in shapes like stalactites. Color normally varies from white to gray, but may also be red, brown or black. Transparent or translucent. Commonly found filling holes in rocks and veins. Flint is a type of chalcedony.

Carnelian, Sard, etc. ▶

There are several kinds of chalcedony. They are usually opaque, but pale kinds, particularly carnelian, may be translucent. Carnelian and sard are red to reddish brown. Jasper is opaque and generally dark red, but may be brown or yellow. Color usually patchy; spots or bands may form. Chrysoprase is apple green. Heliotrope (or "bloodstone") is green with red spots like blood. All are polished for use in rings, pins and other jewelry.

A polished piece of carnelian

Agate and Opal

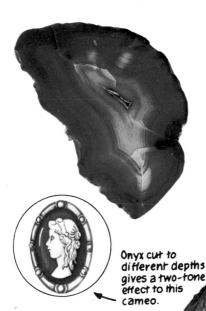

◀ Agate

Agate is the kind of chalcedony which has colored bands. Most agates occur as rounded lumps, from the size of a marble to the size of a soccer ball. Sometimes the center of the agate consists of rock crystal. Bands vary from milky white to green, brown, red and black. Agate is sometimes sold artificially colored. If the bands are straight, it is called onyx. Cut and polished agate is used for ashtrays, etc. Onyx is used to make cameo pins.

Onyx cut to different depths gives a two-tone effect to this cameo.

Opal ▶

Made of silicon, oxygen and water. Makes rounded lumps and small veins too. Varies from colorless to milky white, gray, blue, green, red, brown or black. Transparent to translucent. Precious opal has a brilliant play of colors, usually in blues, reds and yellows. In fire opal the red and yellow colors make firelike reflections. Opal is polished for jewelry. It is sometimes thought unlucky. This may be because it can lose its water, shrink and get lost.

A polished piece of opal

Feldspars

◄ Orthoclase Feldspar

Forms stubby four- and six-sided crystals. Milky white to pale pink in color. Made of potassium, aluminum, silicon and oxygen. Common in granites but occurs in many other igneous rocks and in gneisses. Hardness 6-6½. If you study a piece of polished granite – say on the front of a building – most of the white or pink mineral grains you see are feldspar, and probably orthoclase. Feldspars are the most abundant minerals in the earth's crust. This and similar ones are used to make glass, enamel and porcelain. Also used in kitchen scouring powders.

Plagioclase Feldspar ►

Made of calcium, sodium, aluminum, silicon and oxygen. Hardness 6. Plagioclase feldspars form flat crystals, but are much more common as irregular lumps or masses. They occur in a wide range of igneous rocks and pegmatites. Some are used for making ceramics. One variety (seen here) called labradorite, after the Canadian province, often shows a spectacular play of blues and greens. It is a popular decorative stone. A similar feldspar is seen on the fronts of many buildings.

Labradorite

What are rocks?

Rocks are made of minerals, and usually consist of a mixture of several minerals. Granite, for instance, is made of feldspar, quartz, and sometimes mica as well.

There are only a few "rock-forming" minerals, and most rocks are made of a combination of a few of them. The commonest rock-forming minerals are the feldspars, quartz, the micas, olivine, calcite, the amphiboles and pyroxenes (the last two are represented by augite and hornblende in this book).

Most other minerals are rarely present in quantities large enough to be called rock-forming.

There are three kinds of rocks: **sedimentary, igneous** and **metamorphic** rocks.

Sedimentary rocks

Cliffs or excavations are good places to see sedimentary rocks. They appear as layers of different grain size, or different colors or tones, and the lines of color sometimes make curves that look like waves. These are called "folds".

Sedimentary rocks are formed in the following way:

Rain, wind and ice constantly wear away tiny fragments of rock from exposed surfaces of the earth. This is called "weathering".

Rain washes the pieces of rock into streams. They tumble and knock against each other in the water. This grinds them down into sand and mud and little stones. Eventually they reach the sea.

On the seabed they build up layers, along with the bones and shells of sea creatures. In time, the layers are packed down by the weight of more layers on top. Gradually over millions of years, they become hard rock.

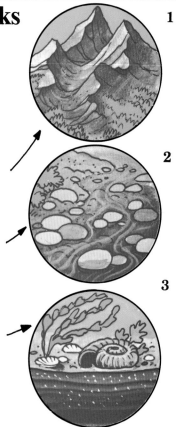

1

2

3

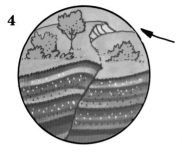

4

Movements of the earth's crust may then lift and bend the sedimentary rocks. It is more difficult to see that a small piece of rock is sedimentary than it is to recognize whole hillsides, because in a small piece the layers are not so obvious. One way of being sure that it is a sedimentary rock is if you find fossils in it.

Igneous rocks

Igneous rocks are formed in two different ways:

Molten rock inside the earth, called **magma,** sometimes gets pushed up to the earth's surface through a weakness in the crust. Volcanoes are made in this way. When the magma pours out above the surface, it is called **lava** and when the lava cools and hardens it becomes rock. Rocks formed like this are called **"extrusive"** igneous rocks.

Other kinds of igneous rock are made when magma works its way in between rocks, and solidifies before it reaches the surface. These are called **"intrusive"** rocks and the individual masses of igneous rock are called **"intrusions".**

The largest kinds of intrusions are **batholiths.** These are huge masses sometimes hundreds of miles across and extremely deep. Granite is a common igneous rock that often forms batholiths.

Veins are deposits of minerals within a rock fracture or joint.

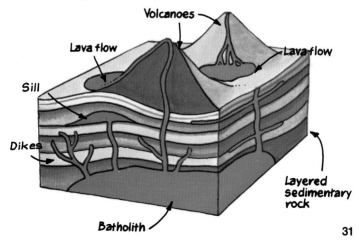

Volcanoes

Lava flow

Lava flow

Sill

Dikes

Batholith

Layered sedimentary rock

Metamorphic rocks

These are made when rocks, often deep within the earth and often around igneous intrusions, are changed by heat. For instance, if magma is forced into sedimentary rocks, the heat alters them into metamorphic rocks. They are also formed by pressure resulting from deep burial within the crust. They may later appear at the earth's surface after movements of the crust.

Some metamorphic rocks, particularly those known as **schists** and **gneisses,** may cover very large areas. They were formed long ago underneath mountain ranges. Weathering gradually wore away the mountains until the metamorphic rocks were revealed.

(View from above)

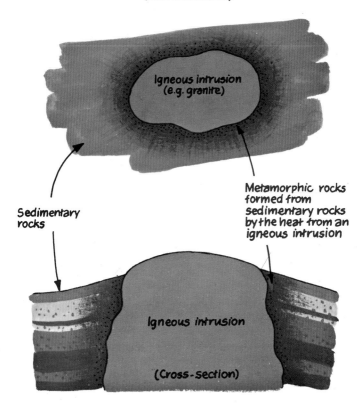

Igneous intrusion (e.g. granite)

Metamorphic rocks formed from sedimentary rocks by the heat from an igneous intrusion

Sedimentary rocks

Igneous intrusion

(Cross-section)

Conglomerate and Breccia

Conglomerate ▶
Made of well rounded
pebbles and boulders with a
sandy material in between.
It may be formed from a wide
range of igneous,
sedimentary or metamorphic
rocks, so its color is variable.
Layers are normally hard to
see, and fossils are rare.
Conglomerates were formed
from pebbles and
boulders washed
down rivers and
along coastlines.

Pebbles

◀ Breccia
Made, like conglomerate,
of larger pieces held
together by finer sandy
material, but fragments are
angular. This shows they were
not carried far by water, as
this would have rounded
them. Often it is formed from
piles of boulders (scree
deposits) along the coast.
Fragments vary from pebble
to boulder size, and may
consist of almost any
sedimentary, igneous or
metamorphic rock.
Layers hard to see.
Color variable.
Fossils rare.

A scree deposit
heaped against
a cliff

Sandstone

"Ripple marks" on a slab of sandstone

▲ Sandstone

Made of grains of sand usually held together by silica or calcite. The grains are often quartz, but may be feldspar or other minerals. Sometimes the grains are very angular, rather than smooth and rounded. Color may be red, yellow, greenish or white. Sandstones are usually layered, though the layers may not be very clear. Layers of tiny mica flakes can occur which allow the sandstone to split easily along the layers. Rocks which split in this way are called flagstones.

"Ripple marks," like those often seen on sandy beaches, are quite common in sandstones. They can mean that the rock was originally deposited in the sea, but they can also be formed by rivers and winds. Most deposits of sand are found in the sea, carried there by rivers. Others, usually red, collected in deserts, driven by the wind. Sandstones are used for building. Glass is made from some very pure sandstones.

Siltstone, Mudstone, Shale

Siltstone ▶

Formed from compacted "silt". This is sediment which is finer grained than sand but coarser than mud. Sometimes larger grains of feldspar or quartz can be distinguished, or the glint of tiny mica flakes on broken surfaces can be seen. Most siltstones are formed in the sea, from silt carried there by rivers. Often pale to dark gray, but may be yellowish or greenish. May show ripple marks or rain prints. Fossils are common.

Rain prints like these are made by raindrops falling on the silt before it hardened into rock.

◀ Mudstone and Shale

Formed mainly in the deeper parts of the sea from the hardening of fine mud. If the rock consists of many very fine layers along which it splits easily, it is called shale; if it is not layered, it is called mudstone. Often black to dark gray, but can be paler gray or yellowish. Sometimes contains pyrite crystals. Fossils are common and often the fossil material is replaced by pyrite.

Mudstone

35

Limestone

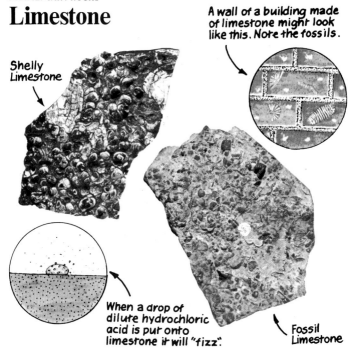

A wall of a building made of limestone might look like this. Note the fossils.

Shelly Limestone

When a drop of dilute hydrochloric acid is put onto limestone it will "fizz".

Fossil Limestone

Limestone ▲

There are several different kinds. Limestone is made principally of the mineral calcite and so will "fizz" under a drop of acid. The calcite may be so fine grained that the rock splinters, almost like porcelain. Or it may form crystals half an inch or more across. Good calcite crystals are found in the veins which often cut across limestone. The larger crystals may be fossil remains.

Fossils of some sort, such as pelecypods, brachiopods, echinoids and corals, are found in many limestones. Limestones can consist of whole coral reefs which have fossilized. They can also be formed almost totally from the shells and bones of sea creatures.

Limestones are usually layered, but the layers are often not clear. The color is often grayish white, but may be black, dark gray or even reddish. They are rather common sedimentary rocks.

Chalk and Oolite

Chalk ▶

Like most other limestones,
chalk is made of calcite. It is
fine grained and usually
porous (absorbs liquid).
Mainly pure white, but can be
stained brown or yellow.
Layers are not usually
obvious on a small scale.
The rock consists of the
skeletons of tiny sea animals.
Fossils such as sea urchins
are often found in it, also
nodules of flint and pyrite.
Its purity suggests that
the seas in which
it was deposited
were very clear.

◀ Oolite

This limestone is made of tiny
spheres called ooliths, usually
about a millimeter across.
Grains of quartz sand and
fragments of shell and other
fossils may be among them.
Commonly yellow to white,
but can be brown or red.
Layered. Ooliths are formed
on the seabed from calcite
that comes from the water.
They build up around sand
grains rolled along on the sea
bottom by currents.
Oolite is used as a
building stone in
some places.

37

Stalactites, Travertine, Tufa

Stalactites and Stalagmites ▶

These are long structures found hanging from cave roofs (stalactites) and growing from cave floors (stalagmites), in limestone areas. They are formed by water with limestone dissolved in it dripping from cave roofs. They are usually white.

Stalactites are often cone shaped coming to a sharp point. Stalagmites are more like pillars. If cut across, growth rings (a bit like those in a tree) show how they have been built up, layer by layer.

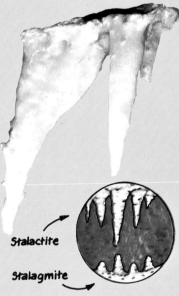

Stalactite

Stalagmite

Travertine

◀ Travertine and Tufa

This kind of limestone is rather porous and spongy. Usually layered, but the layering may be irregular. There may be lots of holes and cavities. Color is white, reddish or yellow. Both travertine and tufa are formed from calcite dissolved in water, so will "fizz" with dilute acid. Tufa occurs in limestone caves and around springs in limestone areas. Travertine is found around hot springs.

Flint and Pyrite Nodules

◀ Flint Nodules

Made of chalcedony. They form rounded lumps which separate easily from the rocks around them. Often potato sized, but can also be a yard or so across. May be roughly spherical or sausage shaped. Found typically in chalk. Flints are usually white outside and black inside. They break to give a smooth, curved surface. Freshly broken edges can cut paper and wood. Used by early man for arrow heads, axes, etc.

Flint nodules showing the black inside and a white outer skin.

Pyrite Nodules ▶

Made of the mineral pyrite. Found in sedimentary rocks such as chalk, siltstone and shale. Can be spherical, but may also be sausagelike or other rounded, but irregular, shapes. Brown or black outside, a shining yellow inside. The nodule is usually made up of thin pyrite crystals radiating out from the center in a starlike form. Sometimes mistaken for meteorites, but the yellow inside makes them easy to recognize.

Granite and Pegmatite

◀ Granite

A coarse grained igneous rock. It formed over a long time, so the crystals were able to grow quite large – over one or two millimeters across. It may be white, gray or pink, but is usually mottled because of the different minerals forming it. The main ones are feldspar, quartz and mica. The mineral grains are all about the same size. Granite forms big intrusions, even hundreds of miles across. Polished, it is used as a decorative building stone.

Pegmatite ▶

A very coarse rock commonly with crystals several inches (yards on rare occasions) across. The main minerals are feldspar, quartz and mica (particularly muscovite), but there are hundreds of others, such as beryl, apatite and corundum. Because the crystals are so large, pegmatites are one of the best rocks from which to collect minerals. They form veins which may be a few hundred yards long (often smaller). Usually found in or near granites.

Gabbro and Serpentinite

Gabbro ▶

A coarse grained rock. Dark in color, usually black, dark gray or greenish. Commonly speckled, since it contains both light-colored minerals (plagioclase feldspar) and black minerals (augite and sometimes olivine). Has an even texture. Gabbro has cooled down from the same kind of molten rock (magma) as basalt. But forming large intrusions, it cools slowly, so allowing larger crystals to grow.

◀ Serpentinite

Made mainly of the mineral serpentine. Often patchy, streaky and veined, with the serpentine forming tiny fibers running across the veins. Usually dark green, but may have black, white or even red patches and streaks. Serpentine is a softish mineral, so serpentinite can be carved quite easily to make objects like ashtrays. Also popular as an ornamental building stone.

Obsidian and Pumice

◀ Obsidian

Obsidian is natural glass formed by the rapid freezing of magma. The freezing is so fast that crystals rarely have time to grow, so a glass (which is really a very stiff liquid) forms. It is usually black, but can be gray. Often evenly colored, but may be banded or streaked in different shades. Since it breaks to give sharp edges and smooth, rounded surfaces, early man used it to make cutting tools.

A broken piece of obsidian showing the typical smooth break, which is shell-like in appearance.

Pumice ▶

Made of natural glass full of tiny gas bubbles. Owing to the bubbles, pumice is very light and will often float on water. It tends to be gray, but may be yellowish. Formed from magma which contains dissolved gas. When the magma reaches the surface (usually in a volcano) the gas appears like the bubbles in a soft drink when the bottle top is removed. If the magma is now chilled very quickly, it forms a glass in which the bubbles are trapped. Is sometimes used as an abrasive.

Rhyolite and Basalt

◀ Rhyolite

A very fine grained rock. May contain a few large crystals of feldspar or quartz. Similar to granite, but cooled more quickly. Is often banded due to flow of molten rock. Can form short, thick lava flows in some volcanoes, or small intrusions. Usually white or gray; may be reddish or black. Can contain spherulites (spheres of very fine-grained feldspar or quartz which grow after cooling). They vary from the size of a grain of sand to the size of a soccer ball.

Basalt ▶

A fine to medium grained rock. Large crystals of plagioclase feldspar, olivine or augite may occur. Often has round or egg shaped holes in it which may be lined or filled with minerals like calcite and chalcedony. Basalt is black to dark gray. It forms intrusions, and also lava flows which can cover thousands of square miles. It also builds up as volcanoes. When thick flows cool, they often break into six-sided columns.

Six-sided columns like these can be seen at the Palisades Sill along Hudson River across from New York City

43

Tuff and Agglomerate

◀ Tuff

Tuff consists of small pieces of volcanic rock and crystals, cemented together into hard rock. It is built up layer by layer from the ash formed by a succession of volcanic explosions. In coarser grained tuffs, you can see the individual rounded pieces, together with broken crystals of minerals such as augite and plagioclase. Sometimes larger "bombs" (see below) may occur. Finer grained tuffs are hard to distinguish from some sedimentary rocks.

Layered tuff with a large "bomb" lying in it

Agglomerate ▶

Made of large lumps of volcanic rock, such as basalt, thrown out of a volcano by violent eruptions. The lumps are at least two inches and can be many yards across. They may be torn from the throat of the volcano or formed from clots of molten lava which freeze when hurled into the air. Often these clots (called volcanic "bombs") become rounded or almond shaped before they harden. The larger lumps lie amongst smaller fragments.

Typical forms of volcanic "bombs"

Marble and Quartzite

Marble ▶

Made mainly of the mineral calcite. Marble is metamorphosed limestone, and the original layering may still show. It will fizz with acid and can be scratched with a sharp knife. Often white, but can be black, red, green or just patchy. Fossils may occur, but are rare. Formed by the metamorphism of limestone near igneous intrusions. Layers of marble can also be common in areas of schists and gneisses. Widely used as a decorative stone and for statues.

◀ Quartzite

Made mainly of grains of quartz, but feldspar, mica or other minerals may be present. Quartzites are metamorphosed quartz sandstones. Usually coarsely layered, they have an even texture and the quartz grains are closely interlocked. Often white, but may be yellowish, gray or reddish. May be found near igneous intrusions or, more often, interbedded with schists and gneisses. Unlike marble, white quartzite cannot be scratched with a knife and will not fizz with acid.

Slate and Phyllite

Slate ▶

Made of very tiny grains of minerals, such as mica, which are too small to be seen with the naked eye. It cleaves into thin sheets.

The layering of the sedimentary rocks from which slate is made can usually still be seen running across cleavage surfaces. It may be black, purple or greenish. Fossils are sometimes found, but are distorted because of metamorphism. Slate is used for billiard tables, roofs and as a decorative and building stone.

You can see slate on some roofs of houses

◀ Phyllite

Like slates, phyllites are made of metamorphosed siltstones and mudstones. They have been heated and squeezed more than slate, however, and so the minerals are coarser. Phyllites split easily into sheets and slabs, and the surface is always shiny. The color is usually silver-gray to green. Phyllites tend to merge into schists.

Mica Schist, Garnet Schist

Mica Schist ▶

Composed of mica, usually biotite, but can be muscovite or both. Quartz and feldspar are commonly present.
If made mainly of muscovite, it tends to be gray or silvery; if biotite, brown or black.
Because these rocks have been squeezed when being metamorphosed, mica schist is often folded (see sketch).
Schists are mainly metamorphosed siltstones and mudstones. Found next to other metamorphic rocks like garnet schist and amphibolite.

Folds like these can be hundreds of yards, or only a few inches, across

◀ Garnet Schist

Usually made of the same minerals as mica schist (above). Garnets are also present. These may be hard to see, or may be as large as half an inch across. They are usually dark red and rounded. Because of the mica, the rock splits easily. It may have small folds like mica schist. It occurs with other metamorphic rocks like mica schist, phyllite and amphibolite.

47

Amphibolite and Gneiss

◀ Amphibolite

Medium to coarse grained. Made mostly of the mineral hornblende. Other minerals like garnet may also be present. Since the hornblende crystals are often lined up parallel to each other, the rock tends to break in one direction. Amphibolites are often banded with darker and lighter layers. They are usually black to dark green. They are mainly metamorphosed igneous rocks such as basalt, and are common as metamorphosed dikes and sills.

Gneiss ▶

Medium to coarse grained. Made mainly of feldspar (white or pink), mica (biotite or muscovite) and quartz. The feldspar may form large crystals that look like eyes. Darker and lighter layers of gneiss often alternate. Veins and patches of coarser quartz and feldspar often occur in it. Gneisses have undergone high temperatures, and may have been partly melted. This causes the veining and the swirling folds that are sometimes seen in them.

Swirling folds like these are common in gneiss.

48

What are fossils?

Fossils provide the only evidence we have for what life was like millions of years ago. They are the remains, preserved in rocks, of once-living animals and plants.

When animals and plants die, their remains usually rot away or are eaten. Fossilized plants and animals, however, have been preserved because their remains were covered over with sand or mud before this happened. In the sea, sand and mud often bury remains particularly quickly.

Fossils may consist of the actual preserved material of the plant or animal, or of minerals that have filled the hole left by the animal after it dissolved away.

Some fossils, known as trace fossils, are the remains of marks such as footprints and burrows.

Fossils are found in sedimentary or slightly metamorphosed sedimentary rocks. Some limestones consist almost wholly of fossils.

If the fossils are made of the actual preserved material of the animal or plant, it is usually the hardest parts that remain, like the shells and bones of animals, and branches and trunks of trees. Sometimes, however, traces of the soft parts too can still be seen.

Dinosaurs are just one of the many extinct groups of animals that we know of only from fossils.

When this dinosaur died, its body was covered with sand and mud. The soft parts of the body then gradually rotted away, but the hard skeleton remained.

As more layers of mud and sand built up, the lower layers became hard rock with the hard parts, or fossil, of the dinosaur skeleton in it.

There are some special places where animal and plant remains have been preserved particularly well. In Siberia, mammoths, which

Woolly mammoth

have long been extinct, have been preserved for thousands of years with the flesh still in good condition. The permanently frozen ground there has acted rather like a deep freezer.

Entire insects are often found in amber which is the fossilized resin of certain kinds of trees.

Fossil ant in amber

The older the rocks, the more the fossilized animals and plants that they contain differ from those of today.

Fossils show that many types of animals and plants are now extinct. They also show that some kinds of animals and plants that we see today have developed only in the relatively recent past. The earliest fossils of man, for instance, are found in rocks only up to a few million years old. Some other fossils, however, are over 600 million years old.

People who study sedimentary rocks and the fossils they contain have divided up the rocks and named them, mainly on the basis of the fossils they contain. These names and ages in millions of years are shown in the diagram on this page.

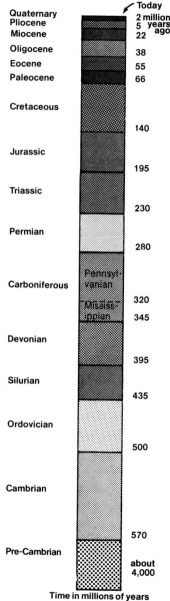

	Today
Quaternary	
Pliocene	2 million
Miocene	5 years ago
	22
Oligocene	38
Eocene	55
Paleocene	66
Cretaceous	
	140
Jurassic	
	195
Triassic	
	230
Permian	
	280
Carboniferous	Pennsylvanian
	320
	Mississippian
	345
Devonian	
	395
Silurian	
	435
Ordovician	
	500
Cambrian	
	570
Pre-Cambrian	about 4,000

Time in millions of years

Fossil Plants and Coral

◀ Fossil Plants
Usually found in fine grained sedimentary rocks, particularly mudstones and shales. Especially common in coal-bearing layers (called coal measures). These are of Carboniferous age. Coal is made from fossilized plant remains. Coal measures plants look quite different from the plants of today. The best preserved fossils of leaves and twigs – even of flowers and fruit – are found in the more recent rocks of Tertiary age.

Coral ▶
These are simple animals with skeletons made of calcite and often preserved as fossils. Coral fossils may be single or in groups (colonies). Colonies may be massive, or have many branches, or form crusts. Many colonies together may form a reef. Fossils of animals that lived in the reef (like pelecypods, gastropods and echinoids) are often found with the coral. Coral fossils are usually found in limestone and some limestones are made mainly of coral.

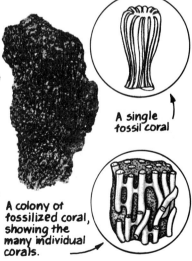

A single fossil coral

A colony of fossilized coral, showing the many individual corals.

Gastropods and Pelecypods

◀ Gastropods

Commonly called snails. They have a shell which is usually coiled – either like a pinwheel, or more often, in a spiral. Spiral shapes may be short and blunt or cone shaped. Growth lines may be seen across the coil. Other lines and ornament may run parallel to the length of the coil. Because of the hard shell, gastropods are easily fossilized. Their fossils are found in limestones, mudstones and shales going back as far as the Cambrian period.

Pelecypods ▶

These are animals with shells, and include cockles, mussels and razor shells. Their fossils are found in shale, limestones and mudstones – particularly younger ones. A shell consists of two "halves" which fit together. They are nearly always mirror images of each other. The part near the hinge of the two halves is known as the beak. Growth lines often run around the shell parallel to its outline. Other, ornamental lines often cross the growth lines.

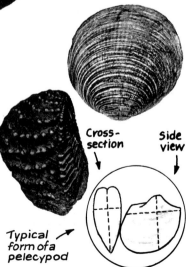

Cross-section

Side view

Typical form of a pelecypod

Brachiopods and Echinoids

Brachiopods ▶

These have two valves, like
pelecypods, but the valves
are unequal in size. The shells
may be smooth or have
growth lines parallel to the
outline. They may be
decorated by grooves and
ridges that fan out from the
middle of the hinge (the beak)
where the two valves join.
Brachiopods still live on the
seabed. They are easily
fossilized. Found in limestones,
mudstones and shales,
especially in those
from Cambrian to
Carboniferous age.

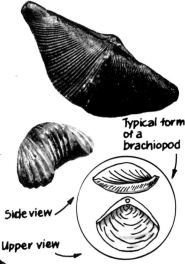

Typical form
of a
brachiopod

Side view

Upper view

◀ Echinoids (sea urchins)

These are round or heart
shaped animals up to four
inches across. The shell is
made of plates of calcite,
often covered with rows of
rounded knobs. If you look
along rocky coasts for
modern sea urchins, you will
see spines attached to these
knobs. In fossils, the spines
are only rarely preserved.
Sea urchins are common as
fossils in rocks of Jurassic
age and younger. Heart
shaped ones are
quite common in
limestones.

A modern
sea urchin.
Note the spines.

Ammonites and Belemnites

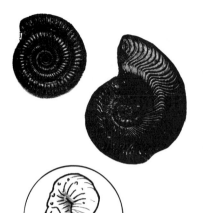

◀ Ammonites

These sea creatures are now extinct. The fossils are flat and circular. The wheel-like shell consists of several compartments. As the animals got bigger, a new, larger compartment would grow for it to move into. Growth lines and ornament often appear on the surface. Ammonites swam freely in the sea, buoyed up by the air in the empty compartments. Fossils are found in many marine rocks, particularly in those from the Triassic to the Cretaceous.

A complete ammonite would have looked like this.

Belemnites ▶

Living belemnites looked a bit like a squid, but they are now extinct. Their remains (once inside the living animal) are bullet shaped with a pointed end. The other end has usually broken off. The break reveals radiating calcite crystals inside, and sometimes growth rings too. If the end is not broken, it forms a cone shaped hole. Some fossils are not much bigger than a match; others may be four inches long and half an inch thick.

A complete belemnite would have looked like this.

Trilobites and Fish Teeth

Trilobites ▶

These animals are extinct. They first appear in rocks of the Cambrian age but had died out by the Permian. They had a head, thorax (body) and tail. The thorax was split up into segments. By moving the segments, some trilobites could roll up into a ball. They also had legs for walking on the seabed. Commonly, only heads and tails are preserved. Eyes may be seen in fossil heads. The fossils are found mainly in siltstones and mudstones.

"Head"

Body

"Tail"

This outline of a trilobite shows the position of the animal's main parts.

◀ Fish Teeth

Rays and sharks have skeletons which are too soft to fossilize well, but have hard teeth which fossilize easily. These are found in rocks as old as the Carboniferous age, but they become commoner in younger rocks, especially in the Cretaceous and Tertiary ages. Sharply pointed, triangular shaped teeth are common, but many shapes occur. Fine lines often run along them, meeting at the point. Shiny, well preserved fossil teeth are used for ornament, e.g. in necklaces.

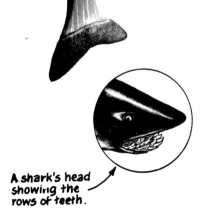

A shark's head showing the rows of teeth.

More about crystals...

When minerals form good crystals, they usually have a characteristic shape. On this page is a selection of common forms of some of the minerals described in this book.

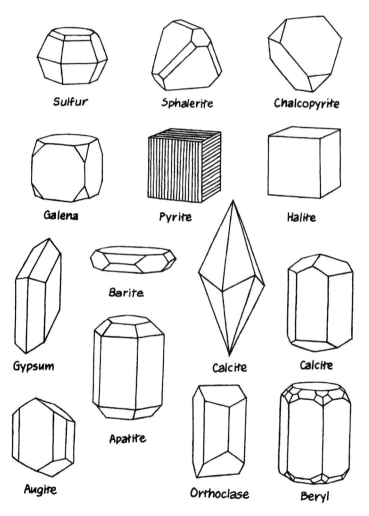

Sulfur

Sphalerite

Chalcopyrite

Galena

Pyrite

Halite

Gypsum

Barite

Calcite

Calcite

Augite

Apatite

Orthoclase

Beryl

...and cleavage patterns

Most minerals split, or cleave, more easily in some directions than others. The breaks, or **cleavage surfaces,** are flat, and a mineral may have one, two three or more directions in which it readily

cleaves. The number of cleavages a mineral has, and the angles between them, are often very helpful in mineral identification. Here are some examples:

Cleavage in one direction only

Mica is a very good example

Cleavage in two directions

This gives four smooth cleavage surfaces e.g. Feldspar

The ends are jagged

Cleavage in three directions

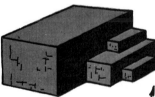

Cleavage at right angles causes the mineral to break into cubes. Examples of this are galena and halite.

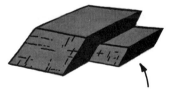

Cleavage not at right angles gives six-sided rhombs. Calcite is an example.

Cleavage in four directions

This can give eight-sided shapes called octahedrons. Fluorite and diamond cleave in this way.

Equipment for collecting

The two pieces of equipment which every mineral, rock and fossil collector needs are a geologic hammer and a pair of lightweight plastic goggles. You can buy them at most rock and mineral shops.

Hammers are made in various sizes. The head is usually square on one side and has either a chisel edge or a small pick on the other. It is used for knocking loose rock, mineral or fossil specimens.

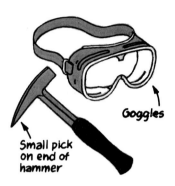

Goggles

Small pick on end of hammer

Beware of chips of rock

When you have found a good specimen, break it away from the rock as neatly as possible, taking care not to damage good crystals, fossils or your fingers. Rocks are hard and can be splintery. Flying pieces of rock are not only dangerous to yourself, but also to others nearby. So HAMMER WITH CARE, away from other people, and ALWAYS wear your goggles when hammering.

As soon as you have collected the specimen, write a number neatly on the back with a felt-tip pen or else press a small piece of adhesive tape on the specimen and write the number on that.

Then enter the number in a field notebook, and write down at the side of it the type of specimen and the exact place where you found it.

You may not be able to identify the specimen properly in the field, but may be able to do this at home with the help of a book or a friend.

How to keep your collection

When you have identified your specimens at home, never just pile them into a drawer or box. They will not only look unattractive but will scratch each other.

The first thing to do is to give each specimen a permanent label, rather than the temporary one you gave it in the field. Write a number on a small piece of white paper (preferably with a waterproof ink like India ink) and glue it on to the specimen. Choose an unimportant place such as the back, never over a good crystal or fossil.

Then enter the number in a notebook, together with information about the specimen. The most important things to enter are the name of the rock, mineral or fossil and the place it came from. If this is not known, write down from where or from whom you got it. You can also record the date when the specimen was obtained. If you collected it yourself, most of this information should be in your field notebook.

> 117 Galena
> Crystal found at Pitcher, Okla.
> June 8th. 1979

You can also make out a label, giving the same information about the specimen as the notebook. This can go in the bottom of the container that will hold the specimen.

The ideal way to keep specimens is in shallow trays, but especially made ones are expensive to buy. Any small, shallow box will do. Such trays or boxes keep specimens and labels together, and prevent them from scratching one another.

The best way to keep the collection is in a cabinet of shallow drawers. Some dealers and mineral shops sell such cabinets. Otherwise an old chest of drawers or cupboard with plenty of shelves will do.

The organization of your collection is very important. Of course, rocks, minerals and fossils should be kept apart. Then each of these groups should be arranged in some sort of logical way. You could arrange them by locality, for instance. Work out a system that suits you.

Specimen in shallow tray

Going further

There are two good ways of learning about a subject that is new to you. The first is to read a good book, and the second is to talk with and learn from people who know more about the subject than you do.

If you are lucky, you may be able to learn more about minerals, rocks and fossils at school. Some schools teach geology and there may be a geology or mineral club that you can join. The club may arrange talks, collecting trips and meetings to look at other people's specimens and perhaps to exchange some of them. This is the best way to learn, because others who have been collecting longer will probably be glad to help, and to pass on what they have learned.

Even if there is not a club in your school, there may be one locally. You could try asking at the local library, or at a museum if there is one in your area. Failing this, you can always start your own club with a few interested friends. You can meet to exchange specimens, and show your latest finds – perhaps specimens you have collected on vacation. You can also lend each other books.

If there is a museum nearby, call in to see if they have any minerals, rocks or fossils on display. A lot of museums do have such displays and they often concentrate on specimens collected locally. Sometimes they have exhibits explaining the local geology. These can be very useful indeed to the collector.

Pronunciation

This is how to pronounce some of the more difficult words in this book.

Arsenopyrite – ah-sen-oh-<u>py</u>-rite
Augite – <u>or</u>-gite
Branchiopods – <u>brack</u>-ee-oh-pods
Breccia – <u>breck</u>-ee-er
Carnelian – car-<u>neel</u>-ee-un
Chalcedony – cal-<u>sed</u>-er-nee
Gneiss – nice

Goethite – <u>ger</u>-tite
Phyllite – <u>fill</u>-ite
Plagioclase – <u>playj</u>-ee-oh-clase
Pumice – <u>pum</u>-iss
Pyrolusite – pie-<u>rol</u>-you-site
Rhyolite – <u>ry</u>-oh-lite
Schist – shist
Serpentinite – ser-<u>pen</u>-tin-ite
Tourmaline – <u>tour</u>-mer-leen
Tufa – <u>too</u>-fer

Books to read

Minerals and Man. Cornelius S. Hurlbut, Jr. (Random House).
Mineralogy for Amateurs. John Kinkankas (D. Van Nostrand).
A Field Guide to Rocks and Minerals, 3rd ed. Frederick H Pough (Houghton Mifflin).

Fossils – An Introduction to Prehistoric Life. W. H. Matthews, III (Barnes and Noble).
Fossils for Amateurs. R. P. MacFall and J. C. Wollin (Van Nostrand Reinhold).
The Procession of Life. A. S. Romer (World Publishing Company).

Glossary

Cleavage (in minerals) – direction in which a crystal usually breaks to produce a flat surface. There may be one or several cleavage directions (see page 57).

Cleavage (in rocks) – direction in which certain metamorphic rocks, particularly slate, split (see page 57).

Crystal – naturally occurring solid substance with flat surfaces (see page 56).

Earth's core – central part of the earth. It is believed to be made mostly of iron.

Earth's crust – uppermost layer of the earth. It varies from 30 to 70 kilometres thick beneath the continents, to only 6 to 8 kilometres thick beneath the oceans.

Earth's mantle – part of the earth lying between the core and the crust. It is some 2,900 kilometres thick and the upper part is probably composed mainly of olivine.

Element – one of the simple substances of which all matter is made. An element cannot be broken down into a simpler substance.

Fossil – remains of, or an impression made by, a once-living animal or plant; found in rocks.

Hardness – hardness of a mineral is a measure of its resistance to being scratched. It can be given a number by reference to Mohs' scale (see page 6).

Igneous rock – type of rock which was once molten (magma).

Intrusions – individual masses of igneous rock formed when magma works its way in between rocks and solidifies before it reaches the surface.

Lava – molten rock which has poured out at the surface of the earth.

Magma – molten rock inside the earth. It solidifies to form igneous rock.

Massive – said of a shapeless lump of rock or mineral.

Matrix – rock in which fossils or crystals are held. Also the finer material between the pebbles, etc. of a conglomerate or breccia.

Metamorphic rock – rocks which have been produced from other rocks by high temperatures and/or pressures.

Mohs' scale – series of ten minerals arranged in order of increasing hardness against which the relative hardness of other minerals can be measured (see page 6).

Nodule – a rounded lump of mineral, found in sedimentary rocks, which easily separates from the surrounding rock.

Rain prints – marks on rock made by rain drops falling on it before it had finally hardened.

Sedimentary rock – rock formed from sediment (sand, mud, animal remains, etc.) on the surface of the earth.

Streak – colour of the powder of a mineral. Made by drawing the mineral firmly over a piece of white, unglazed tile.

Texture – this refers to the relative size and shape of the grains of a rock.

Translucent – said of a substance which allows light to pass through, but does not allow objects to be seen clearly through it.

Transparent – said of a substance through which things can be seen clearly, eg. window glass.

Weathering – the breakdown of rocks at the surface of the earth by rain, wind, frost, etc.

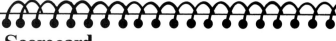

Scorecard

You can score points for seeing rocks, minerals or fossils anywhere – in the ground, around the house, in a museum or store window. Some things, like gold, are hard to find in the ground, but have a low score because you can easily spot some object made of them. Calcite, however, is a common mineral in the ground but has a high score because it is hard to find in the form of an everyday object.

	Score	Date seen		Score	Date seen
Agate	15		Corundum	15	
Agglomerate	25		Diamond	10	
Amethyst	20		Echinoids	20	
Ammonites	15		Emerald & Aquamarine	10	
Amphibolite	25		Feldspars	15	
Apatite	20		Fish Teeth	25	
Arsenopyrite	25		Flint nodules	10	
Augite	20		Fluorite	15	
Barite	25		Fossil plants	20	
Basalt	15		Gabbro	25	
Belemnites	20		Galena	20	
Beryl	20		Garnet	10	
Brachiopods	15		Garnet schist	25	
Breccia	25		Gastropods	20	
Calcite	10		Gneiss	20	
Carnelian	20		Goethite	25	
Chalcedony	25		Gold	5	
Chalcopyrite	20		Granite	15	
Chalk	15		Graphite	5	
Conglomerate	20		Gypsum	15	
Coral	20		Halite	5	

	Score	Date seen		Score	Date seen
Hematite	15		Sandstone	10	
Hornblende	20		Sapphire & Ruby	10	
Limestone	15		Serpentine	15	
Magnetite	20		Serpentinite	20	
Malachite	20		Siltstone	15	
Marble	10		Silver	5	
Mica	15		Slate	5	
Mica schist	20		Smithsonite	25	
Mudstone & Shale	10		Sphalerite	20	
Obsidian	25		Stalactites & Stalagmites	25	
Olivine	20		Sulfur	15	
Oolite	25		Talc	10	
Opal	15		Tourmaline	20	
Pegmatite	25		Travertine & Tufa	25	
Pelecypods	15		Trilobites	25	
Phyllite	20		Tuff	20	
Pumice	25		Turquoise	15	
Pyrite	15				
Pyrite nodules	15				
Pyrolusite	25				
Quartz, Milky	10				
Quartz, Smoky	25				
Quartzite	20				
Rhyolite	20				
Rock Crystal	15				

Index

64